# HAL LEONARD PIANO REPERTOIRE
*Early Intermediate Through Late Intermediate*

# JOURNEY THROUGH THE
# CLASSICS
# ROMANTIC COLLECTION

## COMPILED AND EDITED BY JENNIFER LINN

T0088545

# CONTENTS

*Cover Art: Rose Garden, 1876 (oil on canvas) by Claude Monet (1840-1926)*
*Private Collection / Photo © Lefevre Fine Art Ltd., London / The Bridgeman Art Library*
*Nationality / copyright status: French / out of copyright*
*Adaptation by Jen McClellan*

ISBN 978-1-5400-5314-5

Copyright © 2020 by HAL LEONARD LLC
International Copyright Secured  All Rights Reserved

Visit Hal Leonard Online at
**www.halleonard.com**

Contact us:
**Hal Leonard**
7777 West Bluemound Road
Milwaukee, WI 53213
Email: info@halleonard.com

In Europe, contact:
**Hal Leonard Europe Limited**
42 Wigmore Street
Marylebone, London, W1U 2RN
Email: info@halleonardeurope.com

In Australia, contact:
**Hal Leonard Australia Pty. Ltd.**
4 Lentara Court
Cheltenham, Victoria, 3192 Australia
Email: info@halleonard.com.au

# CONTENTS

## Early Intermediate

## Intermediate

# *Late Intermediate*

# JOURNEY THROUGH THE
# CLASSICS
# ROMANTIC COLLECTION

*Early Intermediate*

# EARLY INTERMEDIATE
## *Reference Chart*

| ✔ | PAGE | TITLE | COMPOSER | KEY | CHALLENGE ELEMENTS |
|---|------|-------|----------|-----|--------------------|
| | 6 | Bagpipe Etude, Op. 47, No. 11 | Stephen Heller | F | Fast and even RH eighth-note patterns in legato touch; LH 5-note chords |
| | 8 | Sad at Heart, Op. 47, No. 5 | Robert Fuchs | Am | Phrasing and balance; damper pedal; voicing; expression |
| | 9 | Tarantella, Op. 157, No. 1 | Fritz Spindler | C | 3/8 time signature; very fast scale passages; legato/staccato coordination |
| | 12 | Theme and Variation, Op. 228 | Cornelius Gurlitt | G | Connecting pedal; portato touch; phrasing; triplets; balance |
| | 14 | Proud Horseman, Op. 47, No. 2 | Robert Fuchs | Am | 6/8 time signature; RH/LH rhythmic coordination; repeating-note fingering |
| | 15 | Spanish Dance, Op. 61, No. 10 | Theodore Oesten | Am | 16th notes; frequent LH shifts; accents; legato/staccato coordination |
| | 16 | Lullaby, Op. 124, No. 6 | Robert Schumann | G | Voicing melody within the RH legato triplets; balance; flexible wrist |
| | 19 | Tarentelle, Op. 123, No. 10 | Cécile Chaminade | Am | 6/8 time signature with fast 8th-note patterns in both hands; jumping LH chords |
| | 22 | Tolling Bell, Op. 125, No. 8 | Stephen Heller | Bm | Voicing melody within the RH chords; pedal technique; coordination of RH/LH |
| | 24 | Mazurka in F, Op. 68, No. 3 | Frédéric Chopin | F | Dotted 8th/16th pattern; grace notes; legato 6ths in RH; damper pedal technique |
| | 28 | Berceuse, Op. 109, No. 7 | Friedrich Burgmüller | F | Voicing melody within RH; grace notes; overlapping pedal; flexible wrist |
| | 30 | Prelude in E Minor, Op. 28, No. 4 | Frédéric Chopin | Em | Dotted 8th/16th; balance between hands; LH repeating chords; grace notes and turns |
| | 32 | Air de Ballet, Op. 123, No. 11 | Cécile Chaminade | D | Lifting off phrases with wrist; reading both hands in treble; D Major key signature |
| | 35 | Etude in E Minor, Op. 47, No. 15 | Stephen Heller | Em | LH melody; coordination of triplet against duple rhythms; voicing melody within RH |
| | 38 | Waltz, Op. 12, No. 2 | Edvard Grieg | Am | Waltz bass in LH; staccato touch; A Major and LH melody in B section; grace notes |
| | 42 | Prelude in B Minor, Op. 28, No. 6 | Frédéric Chopin | Bm | LH melody; coordination of triplet against duple rhythms; voicing melody within RH |

# Bagpipe Etude
## Op. 47, No. 11

Stephen Heller
(1813–1888)

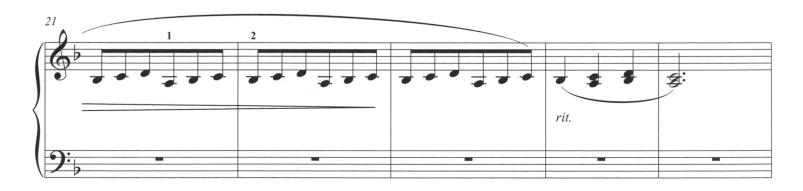

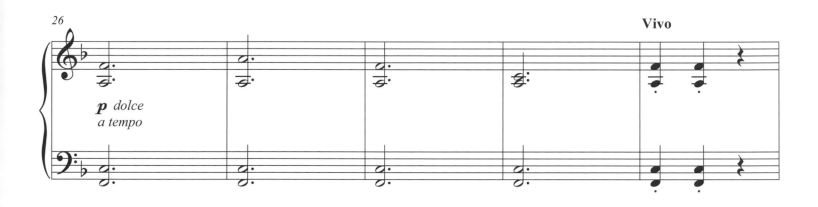

# Sad at Heart
## Op. 47, No. 5

Robert Fuchs
(1847–1927)

# Tarantella
## Op. 157, No. 1

Fritz Spindler
(1817-1905)

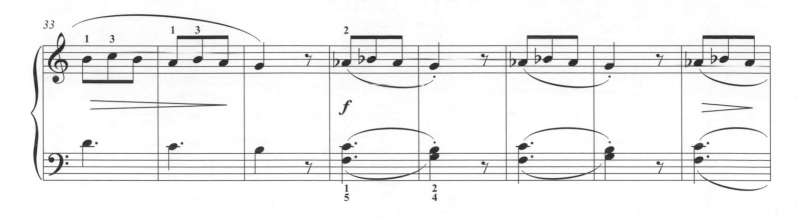

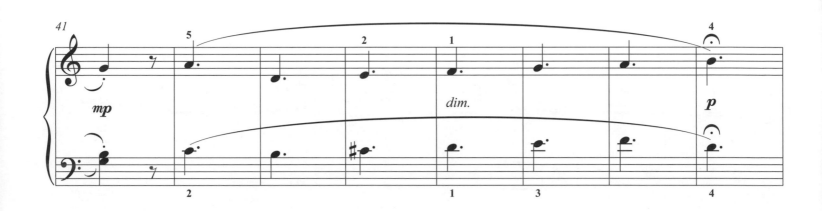

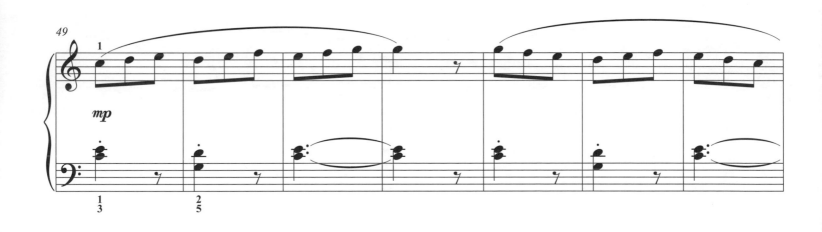

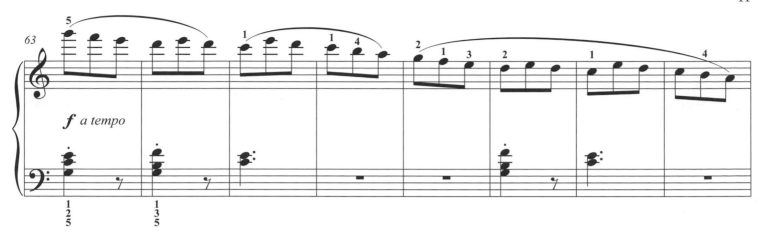

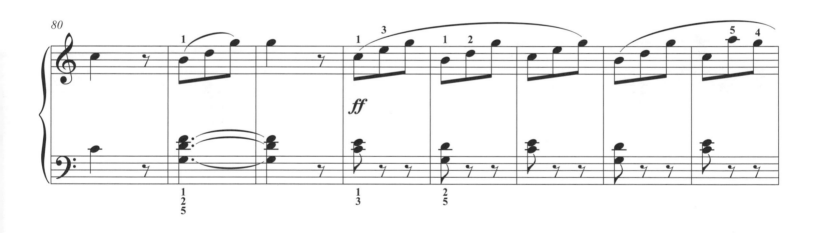

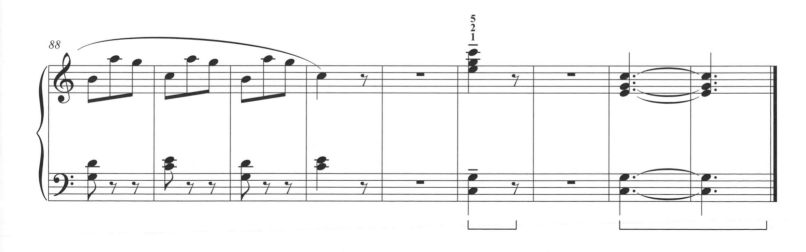

# Theme and Variation
## Op. 228

Cornelius Gurlitt
(1820 1901)

Moderato

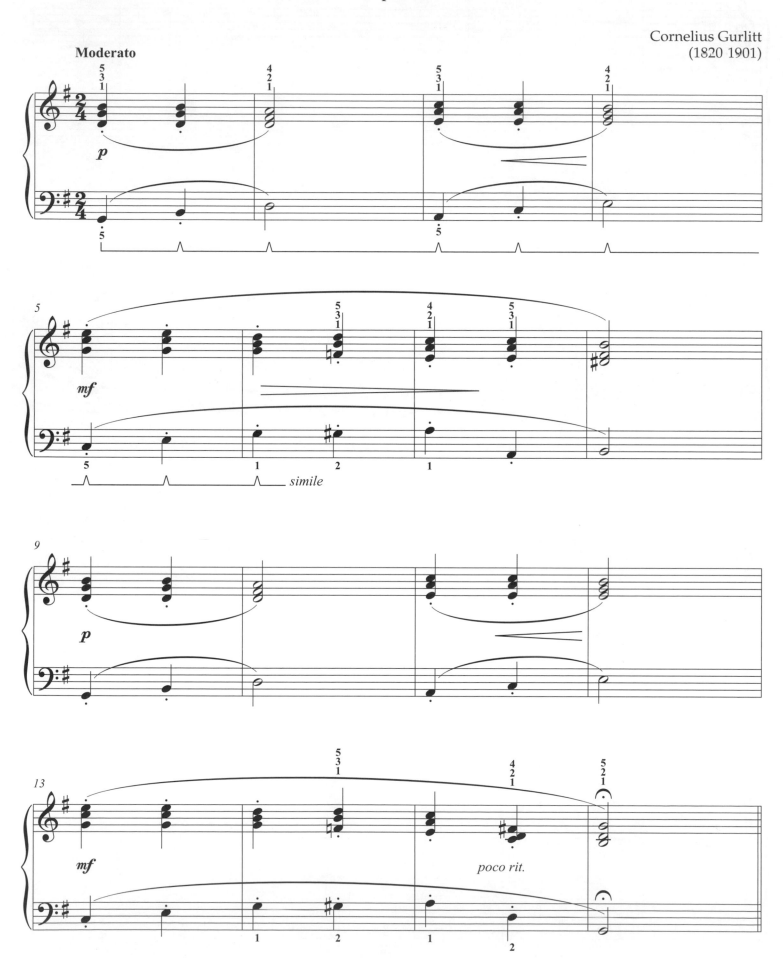

**VARIATION**

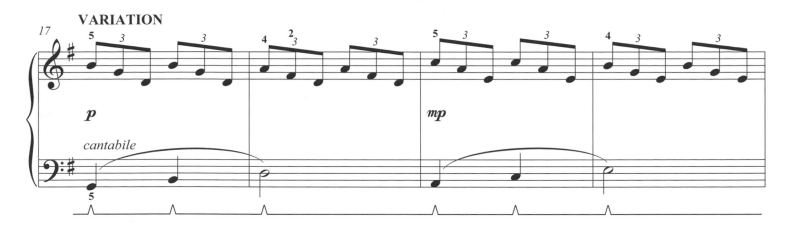

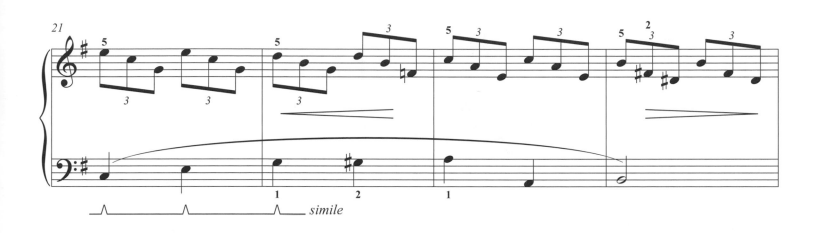

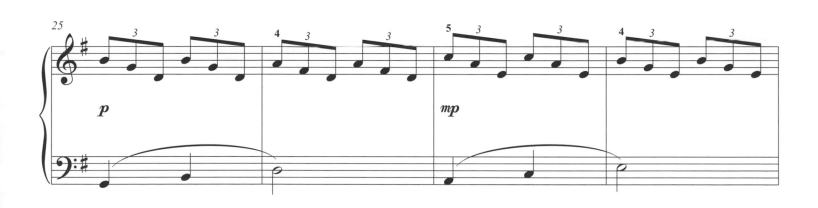

# Proud Horseman
## Op. 47, No. 2

Robert Fuchs
(1847–1927)

# Spanish Dance

## Op. 61, No. 10

Theodore Oesten
(1813-1870)

# Lullaby
## Op. 124, No. 6

Robert Schumann
(1810–1856)

# Tarentelle
## Op. 123, No. 10

Cécile Chaminade
(1857–1944)

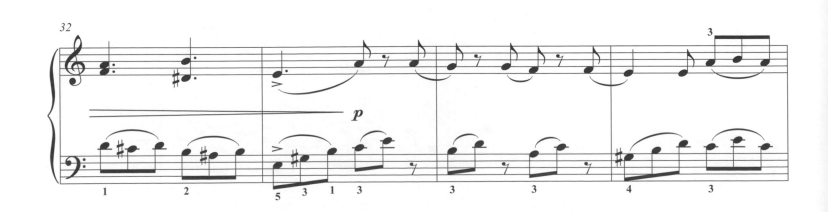

# Tolling Bell

## Op. 125, No. 8

Stephen Heller
(1813-1888)

# Mazurka in F
## Op. 68, No. 3

Frédéric Chopin
(1810–1849)

**Allegro ma non troppo**

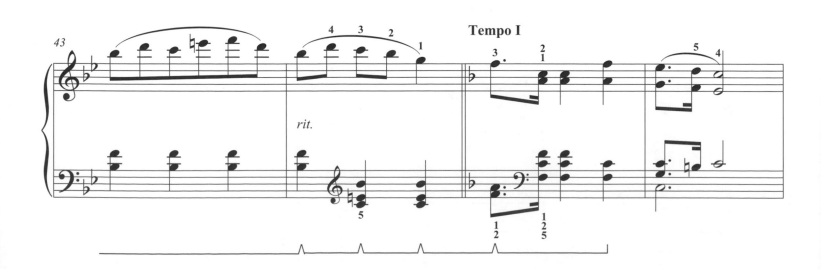

# Berceuse
## Op. 109, No. 7

Friedrich Burgmüller
(1806–1874)

# Prelude in E Minor
## Op. 28, No. 4

Frédéric Chopin
(1810–1849)

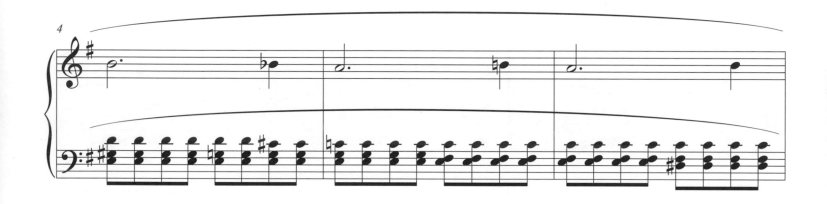

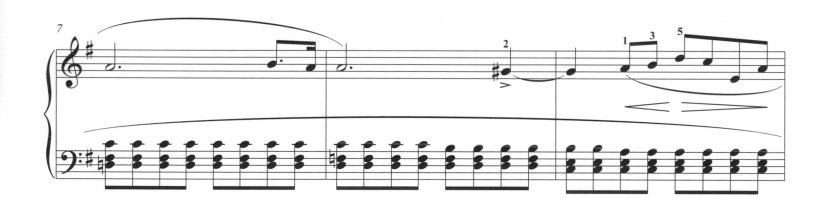

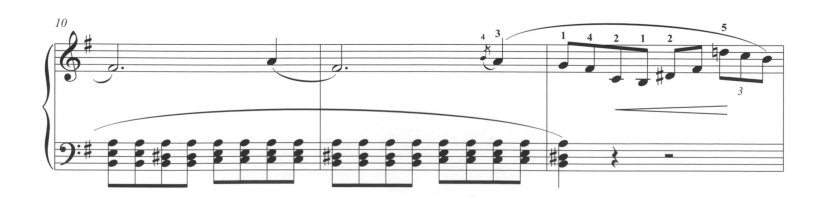

# Air de Ballet
## Op. 123, No. 11

Cécile Chaminade
(1857–1944)

**Mouvement de Valse**

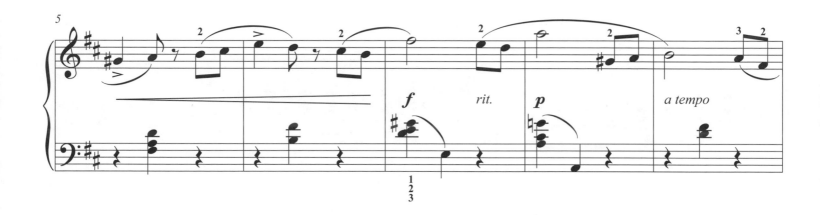

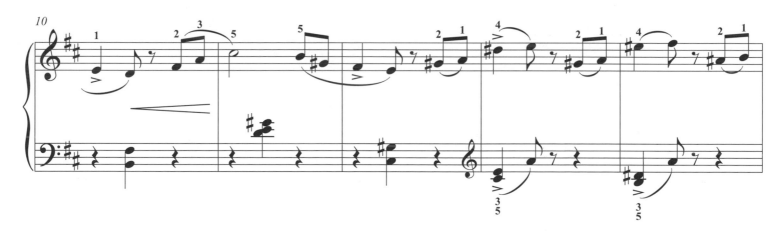

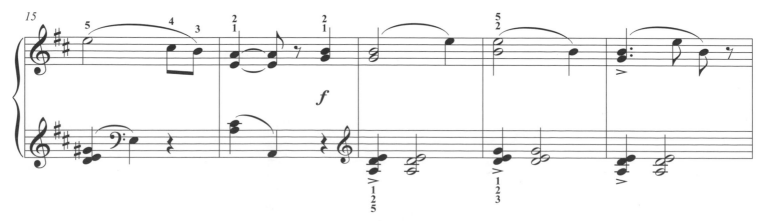

marcato ma
dolce

leggiero

# Etude in E Minor
## Op. 47, No. 15

Stephen Heller
(1813–1888)

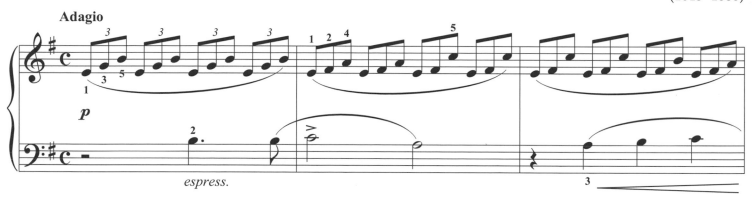

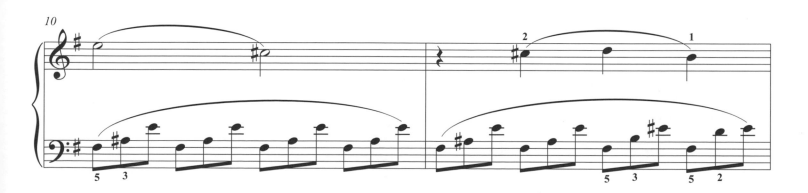

# Waltz
## Op. 12, No. 2

Edvard Grieg
(1843–1907)

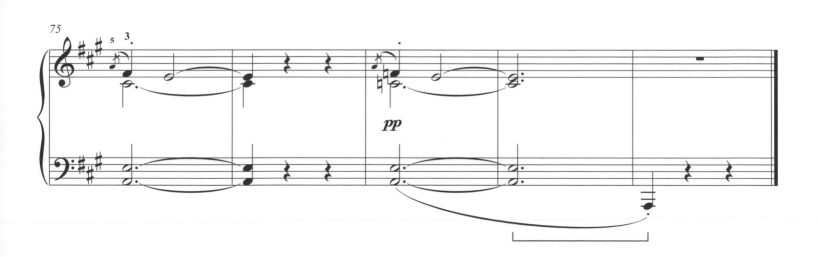

# Prelude in B Minor
## Op. 28, No. 6

Frédéric Chopin
(1810–1849)

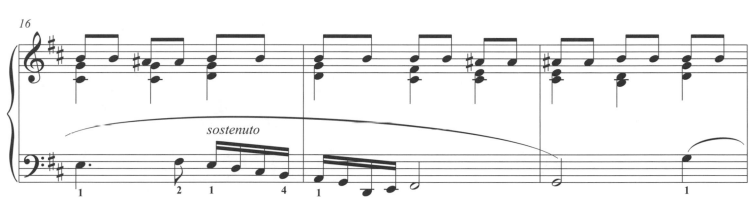

# JOURNEY THROUGH THE
# CLASSICS
# ROMANTIC COLLECTION

*Intermediate*

# INTERMEDIATE
## *Reference Chart*

| ✔ | PAGE | TITLE | COMPOSER | KEY | CHALLENGE ELEMENTS |
|---|---|---|---|---|---|
| | 46 | The Swallow, Op. 100, No. 24 | Friedrich Burgmüller | G | Crossing LH over RH quickly; voicing LH melody over RH arpeggios |
| | 49 | Curious Story, Op. 138, No. 9 | Stephen Heller | F | Quick hand shifts over broad range of the keyboard; precise articulation |
| | 52 | By the Spring, Op. 101, No. 5 | Cornelius Gurlitt | A | A Major key signature; RH wrist lifts off of short phrases |
| | 54 | Waltz, Op. 39, No. 9 | Johannes Brahms | Dm | Careful lift off of short phrases; LH jumping bass; damper pedal technique |
| | 56 | Mazurka, Op. 39, No. 10 | Pyotr Tchaikovsky | Dm | Triplet and dotted rhythms; LH jumping bass; precise articulation and stylistic accents |
| | 59 | Matinée de mai | Charles Gounod | G | 12/8 time signature; fast and continuous RH legato 8ths; LH jumping bass |
| | 62 | Sweet Dreams, Op. 39, No. 21 | Pyotr Tchaikovsky | C | Voicing melody within LH; dotted 8th/16th pattern; syncopation; legato fingering |
| | 65 | Polonaise in G Minor (Posthumous) | Frédéric Chopin | Gm | Quick hand-over-hand arpeggio flourishes; grace notes; balance RH melody over LH chords |
| | 68 | Tristesse, Op. 77, No. 1 | Moritz Moszkowski | Am | 3/8 time signature, voicing of RH and LH melodies; grace notes; reading both hands in treble clef |
| | 72 | Valses Noble, Op. 77, No. 9 | Franz Schubert | Am | Simultaneous octaves or chords in both hands; LH jumping bass; play 2 keys at once with thumb |
| | 74 | Arietta, Op. 12, No. 1 | Edvard Grieg | E♭ | E♭ Major Key signature; inner voice accompaniment split between hands; voicing; grace notes |
| | 76 | Elfin Dance, Op. 12, No. 4 | Edvard Grieg | Em | Precise articulation, dramatic dynamic contrasts; quick hand shifts |
| | 79 | Mignon, Op. 68, No. 35 | Robert Schumann | E♭ | Voicing melody within the RH; dramatic dynamic control, precise damper pedal control |
| | 82 | Venetian Boat Song, Op. 19, No. 6 | Felix Mendelssohn | Gm | LH jumping bass pattern; RH voicing of melody and accompaniment within the hand |
| | 85 | Reiterstück, Op. 68, No. 23 | Robert Schumann | Dm | Wrist rotation in broken octaves and chords; precise articulation, rhythm; dynamic control |
| | 88 | Mazurka in G Minor, Op. 67, No. 2 | Frédéric Chopin | Gm | LH jumping waltz bass; grace notes; RH voicing of melody over LH chords |
| | 91 | From Foreign Lands and People | Robert Schumann | G | Voicing of melody; coordination of accompaniment shared between the hands; dotted vs. triplet rhythms |
| | 92 | Danza de la Rosa | Enrique Granados | B♭ | Crossing LH over RH quickly; careful keyboard choreography and voicing; ornamental grace notes in both hands |

# The Swallow
## Op. 100, No. 24

Friedrich Burgmüller
(1806–1874)

**Allegro non troppo**

# Curious Story
## Op. 138, No. 9

Stephen Heller
(1813–1888)

# By the Spring
## Op. 101, No. 5

Cornelius Gurlitt
(1820-1901)

per - den - do - si

# Waltz
## Op. 39, No. 9

Johannes Brahms
(1833–1897)

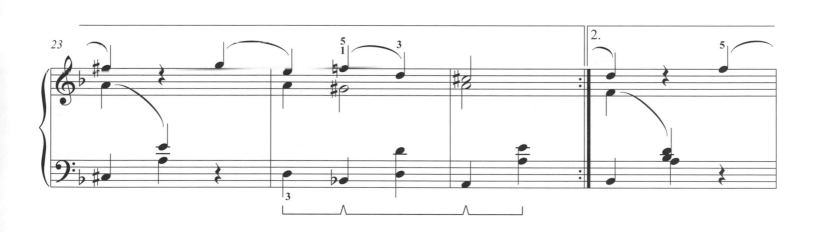

# Mazurka
## Op. 39, No. 10

Pyotr Tchaikovsky
(1840–1893)

**Tempo di Mazurka**

# Matinée de mai
## (May Morning)

Charles Gounod
(1818–1893)

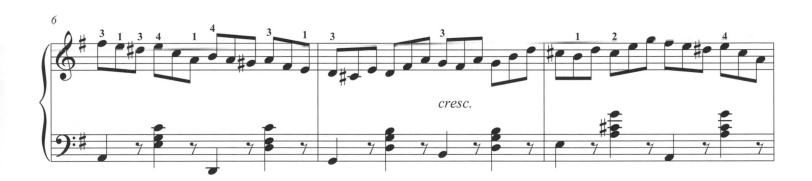

# Sweet Dreams
## Op. 39, No. 21

Pyotr Tchaikovsky
(1840–1893)

**Andante con molto espressione**

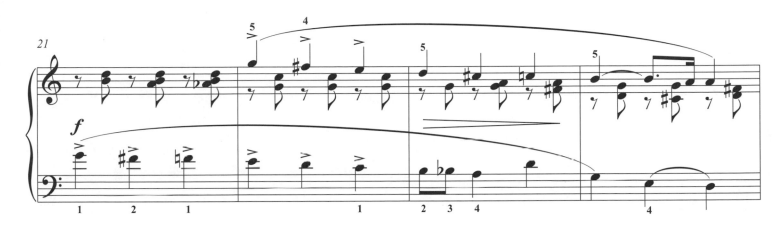

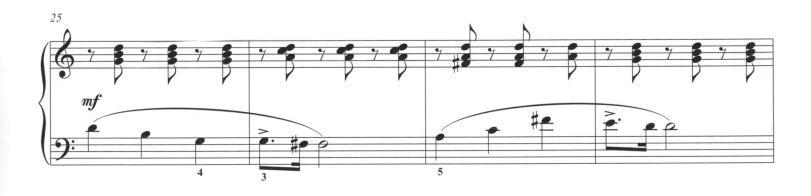

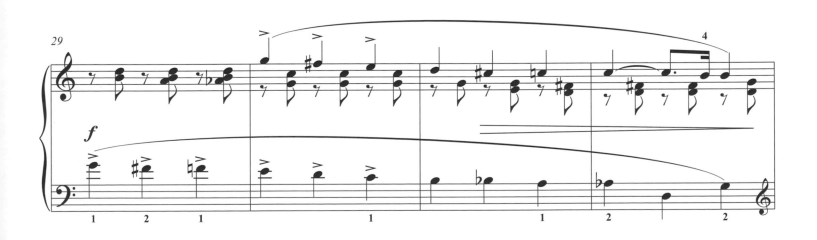

# Polonaise in G Minor
### (Posthumous)

Frédéric Chopin
(1810–1849)

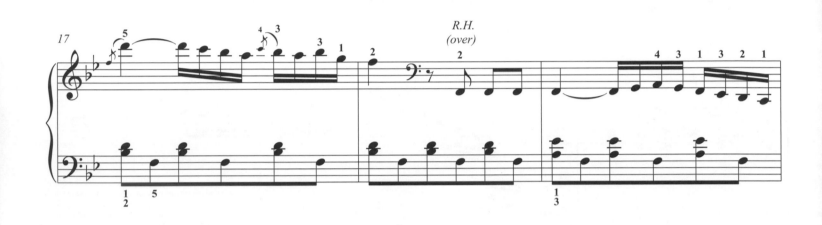

**Trio**

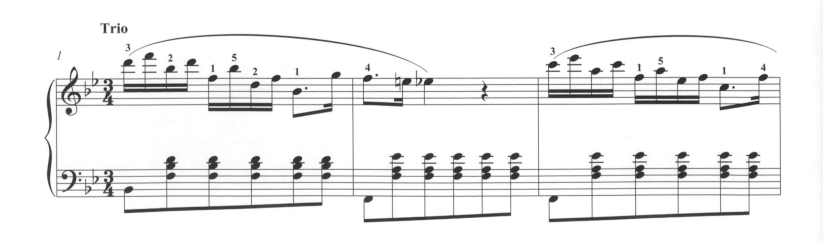

# Tristesse
## Op. 77, No. 1

Moritz Moszkowski
(1854–1925)

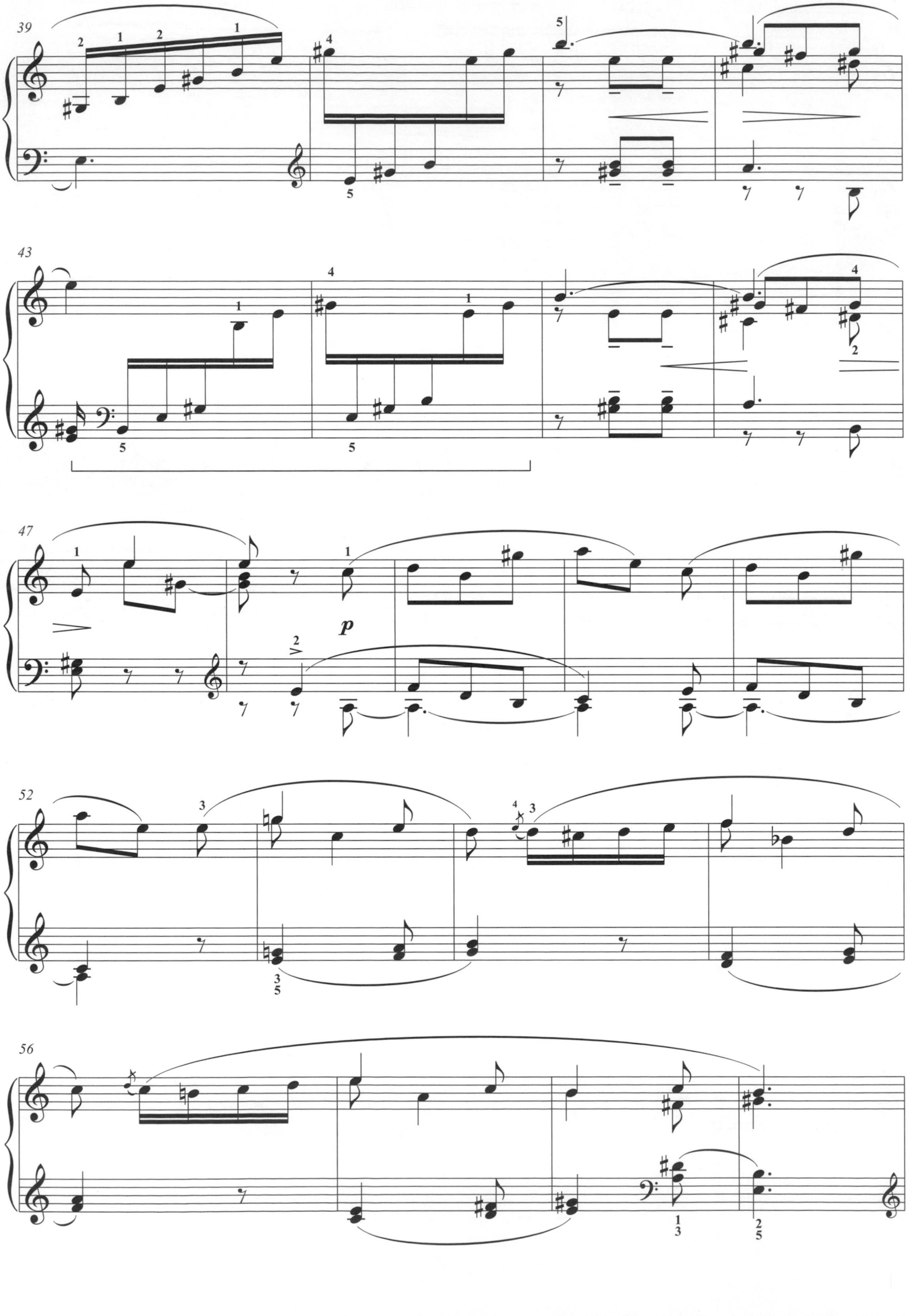

# Valses Noble
## Op. 77, No. 9

Franz Schubert
(1797–1828)

# Arietta
## Op. 12, No. 1

Edvard Grieg
(1843–1907)

# Elfin Dance
## Op. 12, No. 4

Edvard Grieg
(1843–1907)

**Molto Allegro e sempre staccato**

# Mignon
## Op. 68, No. 35

Robert Schumann
(1810–1856)

Slowly, tenderly

# Venetian Boat Song
## Op. 19, No. 6

Felix Mendelssohn
(1809–1847)

# Reiterstück
## (The Horseman)
### Op. 68, No. 23

Robert Schumann
(1810–1856)

# Mazurka in G Minor
## Op. 67, No. 2

Frédéric Chopin
(1810–1849)

# From Foreign Lands and People
## Op. 15, No. 1

Robert Schumann
(1810–1856)

# Danza de la Rosa

Enrique Granados
(1867–1916)

# JOURNEY THROUGH THE
# CLASSICS
# ROMANTIC COLLECTION

*Late Intermediate*

# LATE INTERMEDIATE
## *Reference Chart*

| ✔ | PAGE | TITLE | COMPOSER | KEY | CHALLENGE ELEMENTS |
|---|------|-------|----------|-----|--------------------|
|  | 96 | Important Event, Op. 15, No. 6 | Robert Schumann | A | Quick LH octave melodic content coordinating with rapid chord shifts in RH |
|  | 97 | Song of the Mermaid, Op. 45, No. 16 | Stephen Heller | B♭ | LH melody; LH octaves; dotted rhythms; RH wrist rotation on arpeggiated accompaniment |
|  | 100 | Venetian Gondola Song, Op. 30, No. 6 | Felix Mendelssohn | F♯m | F♯ Minor key signature; LH legato arpeggiated accompaniment; trills |
|  | 103 | Tarantelle | Mikhail Glinka | Am | Wrist rotation in LH broken octaves; playing very quickly in pp with precise and even touch |
|  | 106 | Puck, Op. 71, No. 3 | Edvard Grieg | E♭m | Black-key technique; quick chord changes with crisp staccato touch |
|  | 110 | Notturno, Op. 54, No. 4 | Edvard Grieg | C | Voicing melody with accompaniment within the hand; triplet/duple rhythms; trills |
|  | 115 | Notturno in G Minor | John Field | Gm | Smooth LH arpeggiated accompaniment; damper pedal technique, RH tone projection; dynamic control in repeating chords |
|  | 118 | The Brook, Op. 32, No. 2 | Edward MacDowell | F | Leggierissimo touch in very soft dynamics; chromatic scale passages |
|  | 121 | Moto Perpetuo, Op. 135, No. 3 | Camille Saint-Saëns | E | Study for the LH alone; flexible wrist and finger dexterity; proper body alignment over the entire keyboard |
|  | 126 | Tarentelle, Op. 77, No. 6 | Moritz Moszkowski | Dm | Repeated note technique with alternating fingering; rapid scale passages |
|  | 132 | Nocturne in C Minor (Posthumous) | Frédéric Chopin | Cm | Tone matching in LH broken-chord accompaniment; improvisatory-style RH melody with melismatic flourishes and grace notes |
|  | 136 | Prelude in D♭, Op. 28, No. 15 | Frédéric Chopin | D♭ | D♭ Major key signature; control of repeating notes; tone balance with refined voicing |
|  | 140 | Nocturne in C♯ Minor (Posthumous) | Frédéric Chopin | C♯m | C♯ Minor key signature; polyrhythm coordination with RH triplet against LH duple; trills, long improvisatory-style scale passages |
|  | 145 | Consolation No. 3 | Franz Liszt | D♭ | D♭ Major key signature; LH accompaniment coordination with damper pedal technique; RH voicing projection without percussive tone |
|  | 150 | Intermezzo, Op. 117, No. 1 | Johannes Brahms | E♭ | Refined voicing of melody within a thickly-textured RH; LH moving arpeggio accompaniment |
|  | 154 | Toccatina, Op. 6, No. 1 | Clara Wieck Schumann | Am | Blistering speed requiring flexible wrist, finger dexterity and rapid movement over the keyboard; voicing melody and accompaniment within the hand |

# Important Event
## Op. 15, No. 6

Robert Schumann
(1810–1856)

# Song of the Mermaid
## Op. 45, No. 16

Stephen Heller
(1813–1888)

**Andantino contenerezza**

# Venetian Gondola Song
## Op. 30, No. 6

Felix Mendelssohn
(1809–1847)

# Tarantelle

Mikhail Glinka
(1804–1857)

# Puck
## Op. 71, No. 3

Edvard Grieg
(1843–1907)

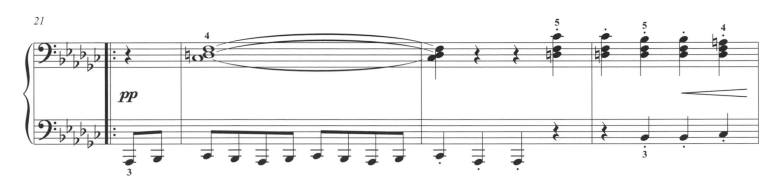

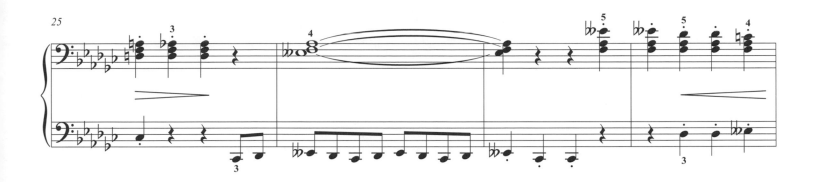

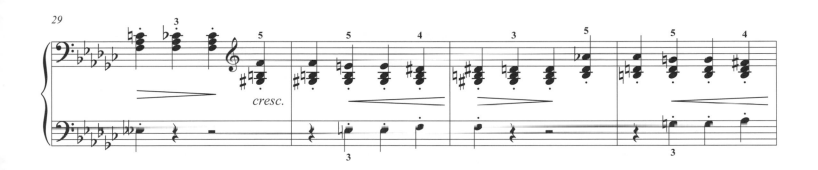

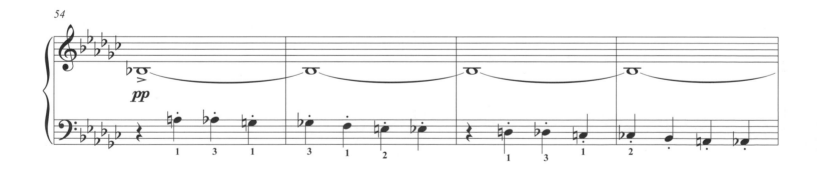

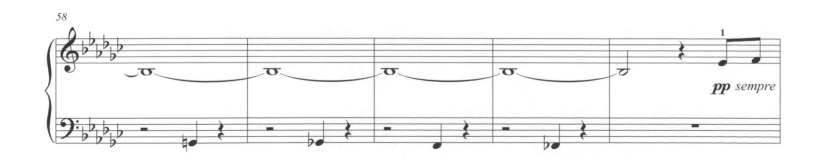

# Notturno
## Op. 54, No. 4

Edvard Grieg
(1843–1907)

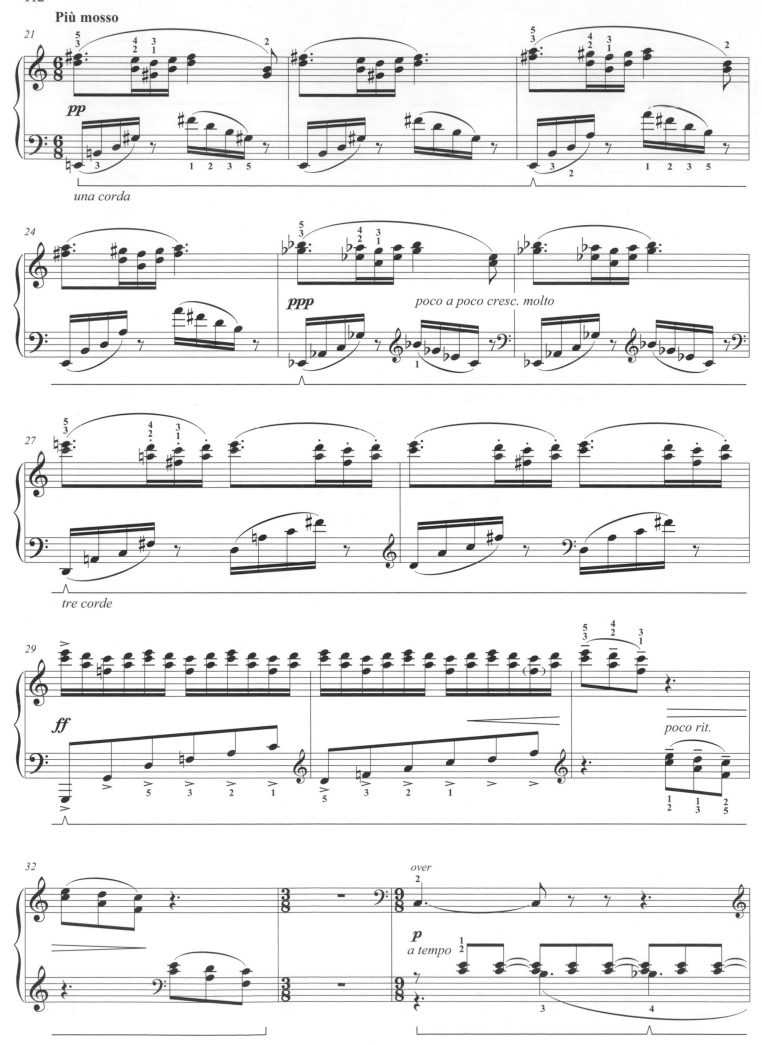

# Notturno in G Minor

John Field
(1782–1837)

# The Brook
## Op. 32, No. 2

Edward MacDowell
(1861–1908)

# Moto Perpetuo

## (Etude for the Left Hand)

### Op. 135, No. 3

Camille Saint-Saëns
(1835–1921)

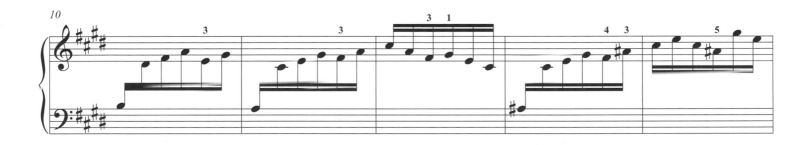

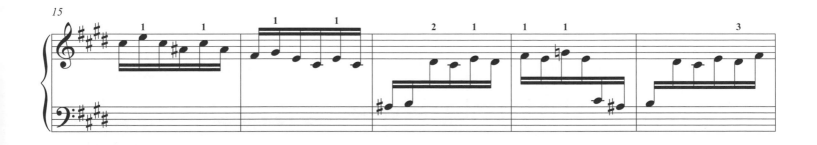

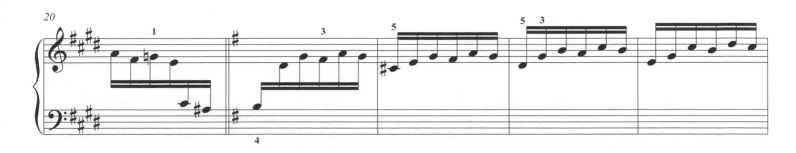

# Tarentelle
## Op. 77, No. 6

Moritz Moszkowski
(1854–1925)

# Nocturne in C Minor
## (Posthumous)

Frédéric Chopin
(1810–1849)

# Prelude in D♭
## Op. 28, No. 15

Frédéric Chopin
(1810–1849)

# Nocturne in C♯ Minor
## (Posthumous)

Frédéric Chopin
(1810–1849)

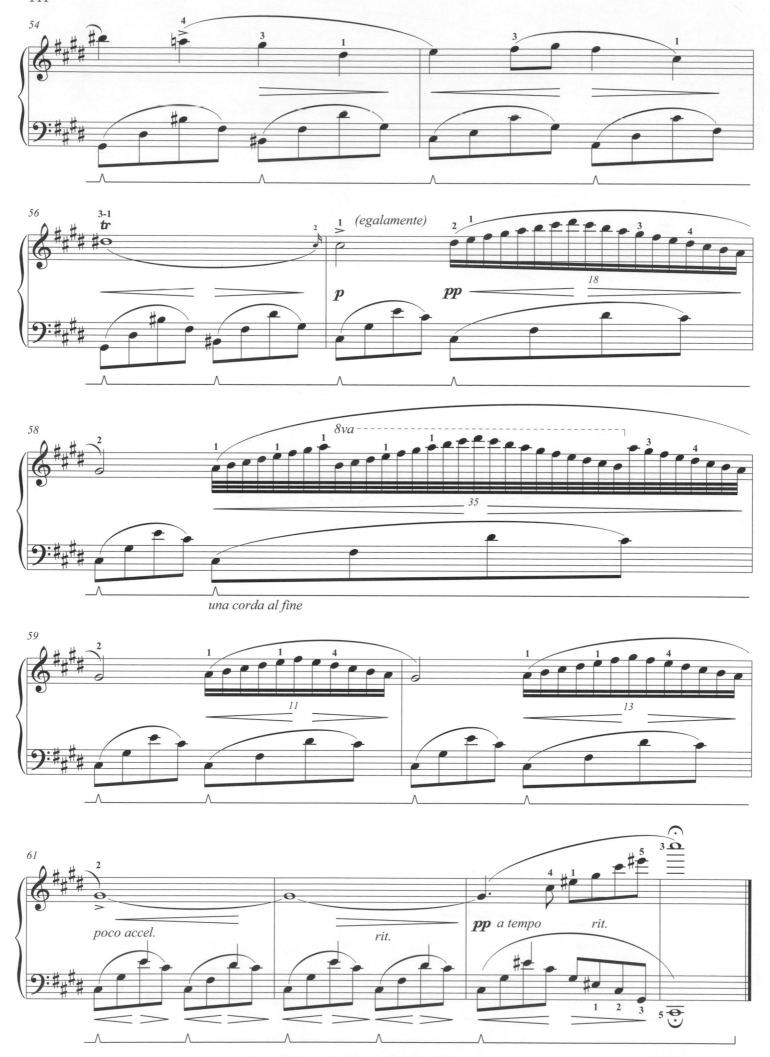

una corda al fine

# Consolation No. 3

Franz Liszt
(1811–1886)

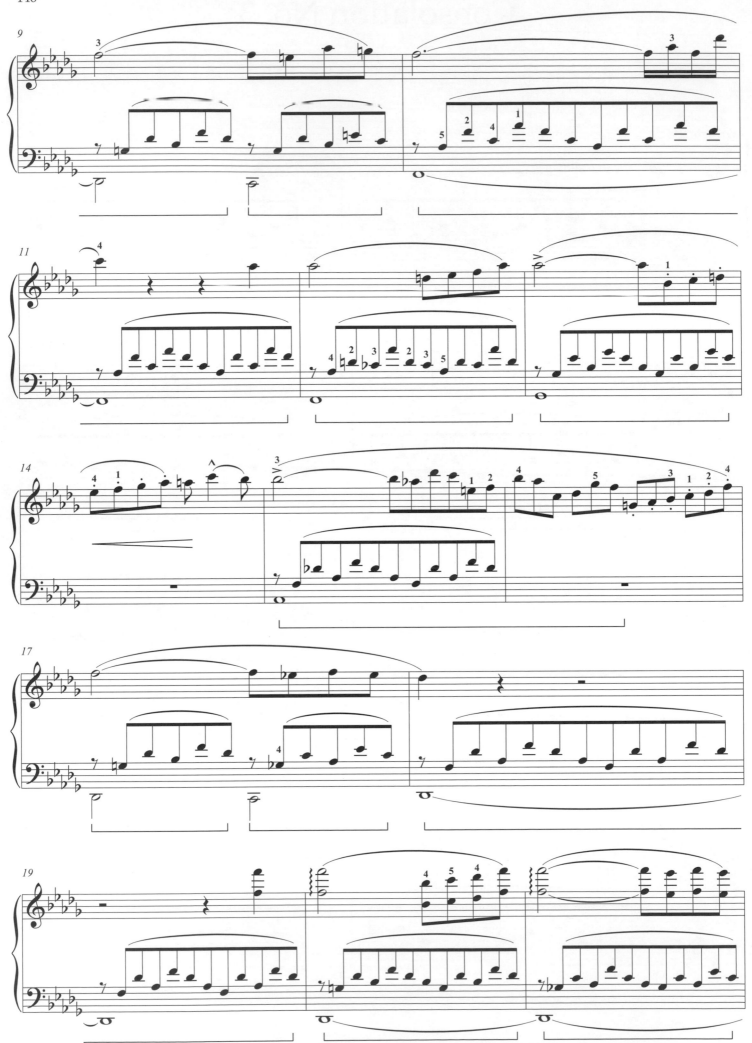

# Intermezzo
## Op. 117, No. 1

Johannes Brahms
(1833–1897)

**Un poco più Andante**

# Toccatina
## Op. 6, No. 1

Clara Wieck Schumann
(1819–1896)